BETWEEN YOU.

FATEMA KAPADIA

Copyright © Fatema Kapadia
All Rights Reserved.

Between you - a poetry book that defines some faces of life that every one face in there life.

Life is all about wandering and emotions which we all feel .

No one can wear your shoes you are the gems of your own .

Life is all about good and also some unseen things .

We all have given this life for some thing so go with the flow.

Fatema kapadia a self made author lives in ahmedabad with her tiny dreams of making this world a happy place to live .

Her moto is to spread love and humanity .

She delicate this book to her mother who had always teach her how to stay stable in life.

INTRODUCTION.

Everyone deals with many things in life.

Some will put you death and some will stoke you at the height but always be careful in both the ways because this both are your test.

As an person you should always give your best to yourself are others too.

Being gentle and good human will be remembered by all.

Index.

Face 1 :- feeling

Face 2:- jealous

Face 3:- overthinking

Face 4 :- pain

Face 5 :- forgiveness

Face 6:- love

Face 7:- god and destiny

Face 8 :- life

Face 1 :- feeling

Its oki not to feel anything. Life shows many phase in some we don't feel anything.

There are no thoughts in our brain.

But it's ok. We move on without thinking.

We do . Everyone has this phase in life where we don't want to think anything and we don't feel anything no happiness , no sadness, no depression, no stress.

We feel like empty body with no soul , no brain , no thoughts all feelings die .

We destroy ourselves from within.

Our expectation are the serial killer which destroy everything.

And in this distraction we feel nothing.

"Nothing can destroy you until you and our unwanted thinking."

Its oki if they doesn't love you like you did

Maybe they had find there soulmate

And maybe you have other person waiting

Love can't be selfish.

If you are in love you will always pray for there happiness.

Tears will fall

Heart will break

Memories will be hurting you like pin

But remember every tear will come back in manner of smile..

Just wait for something new..

Loving someone is so hard when you know they love someone else.

But still to choose to love them.

Love is not deal that should be two side

It's a feeling that you create.

I am sorry

I didn't ask you .

I didn't ask for permission to love you.

But this heart don't know that .

That to love someone you need other person permission to accept you.

Oki maybe there was a choice for you

But for me you were the only choice .

I know you didn't commit but I felt you will

I know you choose me as your friend

But what about this feeling inside we which asked for more.

I know my feelings vanished our friendship.

But I hope you understand that I asked for only love .

Ya I know when you are in that stage where the person you love left is like a
biggest painful movement

At that stage you feel like whole world is laughing at your situation.

Everyone is happy around you and you are the only one which is sad.

You see your friends laughing with there love you see your family happy but you just put an unwanted smile on your sad face.

You hate talking.

You hate going out .

You hate your friends.

You hate everything thing inside you.

Your heart had been like thousands of buried pages.

You suffer.

It hurts the most when you have to sacrifice.

You always ask god "why me?".

"Why you choose me to break why not them"

Your tears are seen by none of them

Not even god.

You feel like not living anymore.

"But remember we all have to break one day so that we can stand up by our own and start new chapter of life "…

Social media and sad song are the most hurtful things.

When you go though heart breaks.

I don't know but every song lyrics u start to understand and feel the same has happened to you..

You break every movement.

"But remember you break you grow "

Sitting alone taught me

I don't hate you

Because maybe you are the person

Who taught me how to love.

Ya I know you break my heart in many pieces

But I also remember you make me feel loved also

Face 2 :- JEALOUSY

Jealousy one of the compared feeling.

Everyone is jealous from the person you are compared with.

Its really normal everyone feels so.

When you know you can't have it and people around you ask for you to have because other have so..

You know every time you did best but always failed in this comparison.

You tired to be perfect but being perfect didn't mean as you were compared…

"Some times it's only us who do this to ourselves ".

Its oki if your cousins are having good Mark's in exam and you are still failure.

I know you had gone though so many trouble of comparison .

Its oki if your cousins are roaming in car and you still don't have cycle in your hand.

I know you have really gone though many sacrifices.

Its oki that your friends always have new uniforms in every new year.

But you still have that 5 years old uniform.

Its oki if your cousins have good clothes to wear of there choice but you have some clothes of others.

I know you really have been jealous of them and ask good to give you so.

Its oki if in school they don't talk to you and teachers don't pay attention on you as you don't take part in any school function

I know you have gone though thousands of broken feelings..

"But remember you have that power which no one else have "

Face 3:- Overthinking

Maybe you think to be happy in your own .

Think which is not going to be true and the best part is you know this.

You know that you can't have that person is your life but you expect by your own that they will be.

But truth is they won't but still you hope and start dreaming.

You think about them while going to bed and smile like an idiot.

You think of them during day .

But the only truth is they are not yours

Let's just stop fighting

Stop fighting from ourselves.

Sometimes you have to do something else

But for others you sacrifice.

You do to make others happy by sacrificing your own smile.

But you still do .

Sometimes you are tried for your own self.

You feel fractured.

You feel unwanted.

You feel no one need you.

You feel like the weight on earth.

"But remember you are still important. You are still wanted by your loved once.

You are only you .

No soul is like you.

You will be happy once again.

You will have glowing face which will put smile on millions faces."

May be overthinking is your biggest enemy

Overthinking destroy your mental peace

Overthinking destroys your emotions

Overthinking hurts you more.

Overthinking can give you happiness of few minutes but at the end it will give you pain

Face 4:- Pain

It take ages to forget

Pain is when they come in front of you.

You love them until you take pain

When you stop taking pain

you stop loving them.

"Its oki to love someone but its not oki to destroy yourself in loving someone ".

It takes lot to forget things

I wish I won't have memory power to remember.

Because it hurt like pin in your body .

And this pin is the hell

And the hell comes in from of tears .

The true thing is you can't fight the destiny.

If that person is not in destiny you fight with thousand things it won't remain.

But if that person is in your destiny they will came back after thousands of fight.

May be god is with you .

May be his decision is right.

May be now you are unhappy,

But remember you will be happy when its your time.

So just trust the time .

The most worst feeling in world is when you are felt by your friends.

The person who use to be in the top of the list

Is no longer in the list.

And you are not of them.

And we console are heart by saying

"Its life it happens ",isn't?.

Some times you want to cry out louder

Some times you need some one by our side

Some times you choose strange to listen your story, our pain .

Some times your feel so along in whole world.

And this some time is your real pain.

Isn't?

Pain is when you do good to other by your heart and they think you are the worst.

At that point you and your soul both gets scare.

Some times you get hurt by memories

It hurts you like pin when you are sad

By remembering old times.

You just want to get back

But time never ever comes back.

You learn by our own mistakes.

I know you get hurt ,

I know you feel is death,

I know you face all alone,

I know you get at your worst,

I know this world has treated you a failure,

But you are going to do the best no one else could do .

Yeah we all learn from our own mistakes.

Its really normal to do it.

Life shows many up and down

Life put you in pain,

Life put you in two roads,

Life is always undesirable .

And the most funny thing is we all are played by some or other game we don't know

The most painful movement in life is

When you want to speak and you can't

You want to show how angry you are but you can't.

You want to cry but you can't because you have been tag with strong human.

But every strong human need a soft shoulder to cry.

Every strong human need a friend to guide.

Every strong human need a partner to cry and laugh with.

And every strong human have a week human with them.

"We all are week and it's really oki you don't need to define anyone .

No one has step in your shoes

So its oki to be week ".

Time is the best healer

By time you forget everything

By time you get up and run again

By time you heal your soul

By time the scare will turn to wooden.

But the pain still remains.

"Its oki if you still feel the pain as we have hearts too with brain"

The real pain is missing someone badly

You know how they are important

But the truth is you have to remember them

And this is because of your heart.

I know it's been very difficult for you to leave them.

But sometimes we can take pain for love.

For them we leave forever.

We never leave loving them but we leave for them .

And that is every difficult part of life.

Cry when you are in pain.

Cry when you are hurt.

Cry when you are in difficulties.

Cry in each sad part.

Cry in each happy part.

Because crying is for you.

Crying is for your heart.

Crying doesn't solve difficulties

But for lighting heart.

Sometimes our heart get too many scars when people around you don't trust .

Sometimes our heart get too heavy

When people around you judge you.

Sometimes our heart get broken by words

That we never thought of listening.

"this all broke us but remember one thing my love it's all what make you stronger at some point you will realize this all don't care you anymore.

And at this you become stronger ".

In pain we all need a strange to talk with.

A strange to listen our own story.

A strange who never judge you .

A strange to cry in front off.

It took years to change yourself from yourself.

Now that the journey from weak to strong was hard.

Now that the journey from best friend to stranger was worst.

Now that the journey from broken to

Fixing self was most difficult.

Face 5:- Forgiveness

Forgiving people are the most difficult task for humans.

We can't forget thing easily when we are attach with heart.

And attachment can't heal by time.

The truth is no time can heal your suffering.

At some point you feel the pain.

The only true with forgiving people

Is to set your soul free for them.

I know you have been hurt

But trust me you will get more hurt

By remembering it.

So forgive and let your soul be free.

Sometime it's not easy to forgive

Sometime you are declare as weak

No one can get you right .

You felt all alone.

"In this you get hurt you get destroy when you want to forget but you can't forgive

But the truth is when you forgive you forget ".

The truth about broken people are

They can heal .

They can forgive hard words.

But they can restore that time.

<u>Face 6:- Love</u>

Love never makes you weak

You always grow and grow in love ,

Because you know they will be with you .

Loving and caring for right person will always

Heal you from pain .

Love never take place with shape ,size , color etc.

It all take place with heart , words, caring, affection.

It always make two different roads to joint for one.

And that one will lead you throughout the life.

The hardest lesson in 20s century is

You can't be main character in everyone's story.

You are the most important character of your own story.

You can't force someone to be every time.

You can't force everybody to be with you all the time.

And this is fact .

You know what's the biggest problem with love.

We always love the wrong person first.

And when the second entry we don't take it so seriously as first.

Why so ?

Love is love first or second.

Who said love happens only once.

It can be twice or even thrice.

The only thing is don't compare any one in love.

Never every because every human is not same .

What if we all break in love.

One day we all will be again in love.

I promise.

You deserve to be loved in all your phase.

Whether you are ice or fire.

Whether you are light or in dark.

Whether you are high or low.

In all the moods.

You deserve it.

I want to paint you on canvas

Because I love you as paint never leave canvas.

I love you like moon.

As moon change the shape

I love you in full moon and even in no moon.

Let's sit in each other's side

And talk about the faults of us.

Because taking will make a way to love.

Being with you can make me so precious

That when I had to go

I can't even take a single step.

Love is for patience

It take minutes to be in love.

But it take age to be with.

Love is not all about taking

Its always all about giving.

Sometime the right way to love

Is to leave .

Sometimes letting go love is also love.

May be this was right to both.

Love is when you understand each other.

You trust each other.

You feel whole.

You feel completed.

Now you don't run for the peoples.

Now you don't dress well to impress.

Now you don't showoff your love.

Now you do is set on chaos and watch movies.

May be right now you must be broken or unhappy

May be you have lost all your Hope's

May be you have disaster

May be you don't feel love anymore.

But I believe in you

You will fight all your pain and try to love again.

You will be smiling face again and seeing you smile there will be lots of smiling face.

Destiny will be there with you again.

So, don't loose the hope my love

You will rise again in love.

Love is not favor for other person

But it's for you.

If you think you love because they want your love then you are not in love

You are just giving favor to them.

Why self love is taken as selfishness

We all have right to choose our love .

Self love is also necessary

Why people think putting our self first is all about being selfish.

Note :- always love and live according to your heart not by someone's mind.

Dear me

I am tried loving others.

Dear me

I am tried putting other first

Dear me

Now that I understand what I want is peace.

Now I want is love of my own.

Now I will not think what people will say.

Now I can wear what I want .

Now I can show what I want

Now I can share what I want.

And people will say me shameless or selfish.

But this is my self-love.

Sometime love is not enough for life

We all loved to stay in love but

Maybe destiny has also some role in love.

So some are still incomplete.

How so where if its love then oki

But when it's for your self then move on.

Because a broken heart will take ages to heal

But a self takes decades to rebuild a self again.

<u>Face 7:- God & destiny</u>

God is a very big creator.

He know what's there for you and what's not.

He knew how much you suffered.

He knew what's the next.

So , if he puts you down then he is going to put you up also.

You can't fight with destiny.

No one can .

If destiny wants them to leave they will leave.

No one stays without reason.

Every one has a reason so they are with you.

"Some one ask me why they leave I did my best then why?"

My simple answer is you did your best but you don't know whether they did or not only god knew this.

And so he made you free from pain .

You believe it or not but life is written by him.

He will do what is good for you .

If he took out your favorite person from your life then he had thought for good.

Remember one thing if he does then he does for a good reason.

Some times god choose you to take a step back.

Because he might saving you from the worst.

So if you fall from top then realize you are saving yourself from the worst .

God is always by our side .

Remember if he removes people from your life then it was good for you and your life.

No matters how much you want them

He know what's good and what's not.

All above trusting people you should trust god.

Because all over some how he will solve everything.

We all lost our Hope's when the prayers are unlistenable.

We all became a hard rock when we can't cry.

But my love once again you will be sand .

And that sand will be created by your god.

It's fine if some people are not walking with you.

And this is for them.

I remember the time we share

The warm and the cold .

I remember the chapter where the hero was you.

If at some point you are no longer

Remember I still think about you .

The time was good but as you are not there I still miss you.

In this life full of lost people good as create some permanent people for you
so keep this people around you.

And this is for them.

No matter how far I go

No matters if there are some part between us.

No matters if I can't sit with you.

No matters if I have never call you.

No matters if I didn't talk about my problems.

But when it's time to go home back I will

Come and stay with you forever.

And this is all for destiny.

I am done with myself.

I am done with my problems.

I am done with my pain.

I am done with happiness.

Because at the end it all about destiny.

And it happens what is written.

So dear humans stop fighting with it.

No doubt your strong prayers will change it .

Just wait for something good don't give up.

-once broken but now healed

Face 8 :- life

Trust the process of life.

Maybe one fine day you will be king of your own kingdom.

Maybe one fine day it all will matter.

Maybe one fine day you will put your self first

Maybe one fine day you will be happy from not any person or thing but
from you.

Maybe right now all will be miserable but all will make sense one fine day.

Some time you just need to leave toxic things

Some time you need to be quite .

Some times you need to trust the things

Some times you need to believe in magic too.

Because it's all about you and your life.

Life could be hard with you.

Or life has give you no choice then to end up

Remember if life puts you in dark then it will put you in light again.

"May this time it would be hard for you to come back again in race but
remember you are the one who is fighting from toxic things alone and if
you can do this you can come back along too."

When it's only you.

You come across thousands of memories.

You came with happy.

You came with sad.

But all over its you

So go with that flow…

That's how life works.

You and me are under same dark sky

But maybe you are with different stars .

And maybe I must be different

But the common is same dark sky which shards us with tears.

Life teach you many things .

But one of this is humanity.

And this is for humanity.

From colour to colour we have changed

From being one we have divided.

From being wholesome we have parted.

And that's not us.

And us is to help each other .

Us is never judge each other.

Us is to believe in each other.

Us is humanity.

In life we go though many faces some good some bad.

Some will break you and some will create you.

Some will be knife for you and some will be spoon .

So now which so ever you are in calm , be grateful, be humble.

Because maybe be this must be yours part but soon time will change .

Because nothing is permanent not even we humans so how can we expect the things too be permanent.

where so ever you are right now stay clam n enjoy life because it's for only one time.

Don't end up for toxic people's or toxic situation because you might get free from ending up but the your own people will be disheartened. .

Don't feel fail if your relationship is not working

Don't feel fail if your work is seen by none

Don't feel fail if you are alone standing opposite to thousands.

Don't feel fail if they cheated on you.

Don't feel fail if they can't see good in you.

Don't feel shame if you have old shoes to start up .

Don't feel fail if you did your best but things don't work out.

Always be sure you are one that no one can ever be….

Every one is not born with golden and sliver spoon .

Some people have to create that spoon.

Because having is good but creating is best.

Nothing is permanent in this world

So how could you expect things to be at same place.

Even the earth is changing its place then we are still human.

No relationship is permanent

No place is permanent

Nothing in this world is permanent expect love.

End.

I hope my words will give you way in life .

I hope my words will give you light and new hope in life.

We all live in society which somehow hurt us or we hurt others but its oki we all do it.

But most important thing is how you deal with it.

In life nothing is permanent it goes some or other now .

So now that I am ending this I have a little request to you all we are humans first so spread love and humanity.

If in this there's any thing which hurt some then I am heartily apologizing it.

All you need to do is be real then being reel for some people .

Contents

Contents

Contents

Contents

Acknowledgements

Foreword

INTRODUCTION.

Everyone deals with many things in life.

Some will put you death and some will stoke you at the height but always be careful in both the ways because this both are your test.

As an person you should always give your best to yourself are others too.

Being gentle and good human will be remembered by all.

Preface

Between you - a poetry book that defines some faces of life that every one face in there life.

Life is all about wandering and emotions which we all feel .

No one can wear your shoes you are the gems of your own .

Life is all about good and also some unseen things .

We all have given this life for some thing so go with the flow.

Index.

Chapter1

<u>Face 1 :- feeling</u>

Its oki not to feel anything. Life shows many phase in some we don't feel anything.

There are no thoughts in our brain.

But it's ok. We move on without thinking.

We do . Everyone has this phase in life where we don't want to think anything and we don't feel anything no happiness , no sadness, no depression, no stress.

We feel like empty body with no soul , no brain , no thoughts all feelings die .

We destroy ourselves from within.

Our expectation are the serial killer which destroy everything.

And in this distraction we feel nothing.

"Nothing can destroy you until you and our unwanted thinking."

Its oki if they doesn't love you like you did

Maybe they had find there soulmate

And maybe you have other person waiting

Love can't be selfish.

If you are in love you will always pray for there happiness.

Tears will fall

Heart will break

Memories will be hurting you like pin

But remember every tear will come back in manner of smile..

Just wait for something new..

Loving someone is so hard when you know they love someone else.

But still to choose to love them.

Love is not deal that should be two side

It's a feeling that you create.

I am sorry

I didn't ask you .

I didn't ask for permission to love you.

But this heart don't know that .

That to love someone you need other person permission to accept you.

Oki maybe there was a choice for you

But for me you were the only choice .

I know you didn't commit but I felt you will

I know you choose me as your friend

But what about this feeling inside we which asked for more.

I know my feelings vanished our friendship.

But I hope you understand that I asked for only love .

Ya I know when you are in that stage where the person you love left is like a biggest painful movement

At that stage you feel like whole world is laughing at your situation.

Everyone is happy around you and you are the only one which is sad.

You see your friends laughing with there love you see your family happy but you just put an unwanted smile on your sad face.

You hate talking.

You hate going out .

You hate your friends.

You hate everything thing inside you.

Your heart had been like thousands of buried pages.

You suffer

It hurts the most when you have to sacrifice.

You always ask god "why me?".

"Why you choose me to break why not them"

Your tears are seen by none of them

Not even god.

You feel like not living anymore.

"But remember we all have to break one day so that we can stand up by our own and start new chapter of life "…

Social media and sad song are the most hurtful things.

When you go though heart breaks.

I don't know but every song lyrics u start to understand and feel the same
has happened to you..

You break every movement.

"But remember you break you grow "

Sitting alone taught me

I don't hate you

Because maybe you are the person

Who taught me how to love.

Ya I know you break my heart in many pieces

But I also remember you make me feel loved also

Chapter2

<u>***Face 2 :- JEALOUSY***</u>

Jealousy one of the compared feeling.

Everyone is jealous from the person you are compared with.

Its really normal everyone feels so.

When you know you can't have it and people around you ask for you to have because other have so..

You know every time you did best but always failed in this comparison.

You tired to be perfect but being perfect didn't mean as you were compared…

"Some times it's only us who do this to ourselves ".

Its oki if your cousins are having good Mark's in exam and you are still failure.

I know you had gone though so many trouble of comparison .

Its oki if your cousins are roaming in car and you still don't have cycle in your hand.

I know you have really gone though many sacrifices.

Its oki that your friends always have new uniforms in every new year.

But you still have that 5 years old uniform.

Its oki if your cousins have good clothes to wear of there choice but you have some clothes of others.

I know you really have been jealous of them and ask good to give you so.

Its oki if in school they don't talk to you and teachers don't pay attention on you as you don't take part in any school function

I know you have gone though thousands of broken feelings..

"But remember you have that power which no one else have "

Chapter3

Face 3:- overthing.

Maybe you think to be happy in your own .

Think which is not going to be true and the best part is you know this.

You know that you can't have that person is your life but you expect by your own that they will be.

But truth is they won't but still you hope and start dreaming.

You think about them while going to bed and smile like an idiot.

You think of them during day .

But the only truth is they are not yours

Let's just stop fighting

Stop fighting from ourselves.

Sometimes you have to do something else

But for others you sacrifice.

You do to make others happy by sacrificing your own smile.

But you still do .

Sometimes you are tried for your own self.

You feel fractured.

You feel unwanted.

You feel no one need you.

You feel like the weight on earth.

"But remember you are still important. You are still wanted by your loved once.

You are only you .

No soul is like you.

You will be happy once again.

You will have glowing face which will put smile on millions faces."

May be overthinking is your biggest enemy

Overthinking destroy your mental peace

Overthinking destroys your emotions

Overthinking hurts you more.

Overthinking can give you happiness of few minutes but at the end it will give you pain

Chapter4

<u>*Face 4 :- Pain*</u>

It take ages to forget

Pain is when they come in front of you.

You love them until you take pain

When you stop taking pain

you stop loving them.

"Its oki to love someone but its not oki to destroy yourself in loving
someone ".

It takes lot to forget things

I wish I won't have memory power to remember.

Because it hurt like pin in your body .

And this pin is the hell

And the hell comes in from of tears .

The true thing is you can't fight the destiny.

If that person is not in destiny you fight with thousand things it won't remain.

But if that person is in your destiny they will came back after thousands of fight.

May be god is with you .

May be his decision is right.

May be now you are unhappy,

But remember you will be happy when its your time.

So just trust the time .

The most worst feeling in world is when you are felt by your friends.

The person who use to be in the top of the list

Is no longer in the list.

And you are not of them.

And we console are heart by saying

"Its life it happens ",isn't?.

Some times you want to cry out louder

Some times you need some one by our side

Some times you choose strange to listen your story, our pain .

Some times your feel so along in whole world.

And this some time is your real pain.

Isn't?

Pain is when you do good to others by ypur heart and they think you are

worst .

At that point you and your soul both gets scare.

Some times you get hurt by memories

It hurts you like pin when you are sad

By remembering old times.

You just want to get back

But time never ever comes back.

You learn by our own mistakes.

I know you get hurt ,

I know you feel is death,

I know you face all alone,

I know you get at your worst,

I know this world has treated you a failure,

But you are going to do the best no one else could do .

Yeah we all learn from our own mistakes.

Its really normal to do it.

Life shows many up and down

Life put you in pain,

Life put you in two roads,

Life is always undesirable .

And the most funny thing is we all are played by some or other game we
don't know

The most painful movement in life is

When you want to speak and you can't

You want to show how angry you are but you can't.

You want to cry but you can't because you have been tag with strong
human.

But every strong human need a soft shoulder to cry.

Every strong human need a friend to guide.

Every strong human need a partner to cry and laugh with.

And every strong human have a week human with them.

"We all are week and it's really oki you don't need to define anyone .

No one has step in your shoes

So its oki to be week "

Time is the best healer

By time you forget everything

By time you get up and run again

By time you heal your soul

By time the scare will turn to wooden.

But the pain still remains.

"Its oki if you still feel the pain as we have hearts too with brain"

I know it's been very difficult for you to leave them.

But sometimes we can take pain for love.

For them we leave forever.

We never leave loving them but we leave for them .

And that is every difficult part of life.

Cry when you are in pain.

Cry when you are hurt.

Cry when you are in difficulties.

Cry in each sad part.

Cry in each happy part.

Because crying is for you.

Crying is for your heart.

Crying doesn't solve difficulties

But for lighting heart.

sometimes our heart get too many scars when people around you don't trust

.

Sometimes our heart get too heavy

When people around you judge you.

Sometimes our heart get broken by words

That we never thought of listening.

"this all broke us but remember one thing my love it's all what make you stronger at some point you will realize this all don't care you anymore.

And at this you become stronger ".

In pain we all need a strange to talk with.

A strange to listen our own story.

A strange who never judge you .

A strange to cry in front off.

It took years to change yourself from yourself.

Now that the journey from weak to strong was hard.

Now that the journey from best friend to stranger was worst.

Now that the journey from broken to

Fixing self was most difficult.

The real pain is missing someone badly

You know how they are important

But the truth is you have to remember them

And this is because of your heart.

Chapter5

<u>*Face 5:-Love*</u>

Being with you can make me so precious

That when I had to go

I can't even take a single step.

Love is for patience

It take minutes to be in love.

But it take age to be with.

Love is not all about taking

Its always all about giving.

Sometime the right way to love

Is to leave .

Sometimes letting go love is also love.

May be this was right to both.

Love is when you understand each other.

You trust each other.

You feel whole.

You feel completed.

Now you don't run for the peoples.

Now you don't dress well to impress.

Now you don't showoff your love.

Now you do is set on chaos and watch movies.

May be right now you must be broken or unhappy

May be you have lost all your Hope's

May be you have disaster

May be you don't feel love anymore.

But I believe in you

You will fight all your pain and try to love again.

You will be smiling face again and seeing you smile there will be lots of smiling face.

Destiny will be there with you again.

So, don't loose the hope my love

You will rise again in love.

Love is not favor for other person

But it's for you.

If you think you love because they want your love then you are not in love

You are just giving favor to them.

Why self love is taken as selfishness

We all have right to choose our love .

Self love is also necessary

Why people think putting our self first is all about being selfish.

Note :- always love and live according to your heart not by someone's mind.

Dear me

I am tried loving others.

Dear me

I am tried putting other first

Dear me

Now that I understand what I want is peace.

Now I want is love of my own.

Now I will not think what people will say.

Now I can wear what I want .

Now I can show what I want

Now I can share what I want.

And people will say me shameless or selfish.

But this is my self-love.

May be right now you must be broken or unhappy

May be you have lost all your Hope's

May be you have disaster

May be you don't feel love anymore.

But I believe in you

You will fight all your pain and try to love again.

You will be smiling face again and seeing you smile there will be lots of
smiling face.

Destiny will be there with you again.

So, don't loose the hope my love

You will rise again in love.

Love is not favor for other person

But it's for you.

If you think you love because they want your love then you are not in love

You are just giving favor to them.

"Some one ask me why they leave I did my best then why?"

My simple answer is you did your best but you don't know whether they
did or not only god knew this.

And so he made you free from pain .

Love never makes you weak

You always grow and grow in love ,

Because you know they will be with you .

Loving and caring for right person will always

Heal you from pain .

Love never take place with shape ,size , color etc.

It all take place with heart , words, caring, affection.

It always make two different roads to joint for one.

And that one will lead you throughout the life.

The hardest lesson in 20s century is

You can't be main character in everyone's story.

You are the most important character of your own story.

You can't force someone to be every time.

You can't force everybody to be with you all the time.

And this is fact .

You know what's the biggest problem with love.

We always love the wrong person first.

And when the second entry we don't take it so seriously as first.

Why so ?

Love is love first or second.

Who said love happens only once.

It can be twice or even thrice.

The only thing is don't compare any one in love.

Never every because every human is not same .

What if we all break in love.

One day we all will be again in love.

I promise.

You deserve to be loved in all your phase.

Whether you are ice or fire.

Whether you are light or in dark.

Whether you are high or low.

In all the moods.

You deserve it.

I want to paint you on canvas

Because I love you as paint never leave canvas.

I love you like moon.

As moon change the shape

I love you in full moon and even in no moon.

Why self love is taken as selfishness

We all have right to choose our love .

Self love is also necessary

Why people think putting our self first is all about being selfish.

Note :- always love and live according to your heart not by someone's mind.

Note :- always love and live according to your heart not by someone's mind.

Let's sit in each other's side

And talk about the faults of us.

Because taking will make a way to love.

Chapter6

<u>Face 6 :- Forgiviness</u>

Sometime it's not easy to forgive

Sometime you are declare as weak

No one can get you right .

You felt all alone.

"In this you get hurt you get destroy when you want to forget but you can't forgive

But the truth is when you forgive you forget ".

Forgiving people are the most difficult task for humans.

We can't forget thing easily when we are attach with heart.

And attachment can't heal by time.

The truth is no time can heal your suffering.

At some point you feel the pain.

The truth about broken people are

They can heal .

They can forgive hard words.

But they can restore that time.

The only true with forgiving people

Is to set your soul free for them.

I know you have been hurt

But trust me you will get more hurt

By remembering it.

So forgive and let your soul be free.

Chapter 7

Face 7:-God N Destiny

You can't fight with destiny.

No one can .

If destiny wants them to leave they will leave.

No one stays without reason.

Every one has a reason so they are with you.

You believe it or not but life is written by him.

He will do what is good for you .

If he took out your favorite person from your life then he had thought for good.

Remember one thing if he does then he does for a good reason.

God is always by our side .

Remember if he removes people from your life then it was good for you and
your life.

No matters how much you want them

He know what's good and what's not.

Some times god choose you to take a step back.

Because he might saving you from the worst.

So if you fall from top then realize you are saving yourself from the worst .

All above trusting people you should trust god.

Because all over some how he will solve everything.

We all lost our Hope's when the prayers are unlistenable.

We all became a hard rock when we can't cry.

But my love once again you will be sand .

And that sand will be created by your god.

It's fine if some people are not walking with you.

And this is for them.

I remember the time we share

The warm and the cold .

I remember the chapter where the hero was you.

If at some point you are no longer

Remember I still think about you .

The time was good but as you are not there I still miss you.

In this life full of lost people good as create some permanent people for you

so keep this people around you.

And this is for them.

No matter how far I go

No matters if there are some part between us.

No matters if I can't sit with you.

No matters if I have never call you.

No matters if I didn't talk about my problems.

But when it's time to go home back I will

Come and stay with you forever.

And this is all for destiny.

I am done with myself.

I am done with my problems.

I am done with my pain.

I am done with happiness.

Because at the end it all about destiny.

And it happens what is written.

So dear humans stop fighting with it.

No doubt your strong prayers will change it

Because at the end it all about destiny.

And it happens what is written.

So dear humans stop fighting with it.

No doubt your strong prayers will change it .

Just wait for something good don't give up.

-once broken but now healed

Face 8 :- life

Trust the process of life.

Maybe one fine day you will be king of your own kingdom.

Maybe one fine day it all will matter.

Maybe one fine day you will put your self first

Maybe one fine day you will be happy from not any person or thing but from you.

Maybe right now all will be miserable but all will make sense one fine day.

Some time you just need to leave toxic things

Some time you need to be quite .

Some times you need to trust the things

Some times you need to believe in magic too.

Because it's all about you and your life.

Life could be hard with you.

Or life has give you no choice then to end up

Remember if life puts you in dark then it will put you in light again.

"May this time it would be hard for you to come back again in race but

remember you are the one who is fighting from toxic things alone and if

you can do this you can come back along too."

When it's only you.

You come across thousands of memories.

You came with happy.

You came with sad.

But all over its you

So go with that flow…

That's how life works

You and me are under same dark sky

But maybe you are with different stars .

And maybe I must be different

But the common is same dark sky which shards us with tears.

Life teach you many things .

But one of this is humanity.

And this is for humanity.

From colour to colour we have changed

From being one we have divided.

From being wholesome we have parted.

And that's not us.

And us is to help each other .

Us is never judge each other.

Us is to believe in each other.

Us is humanity.

In life we go though many faces some good some bad.

Some will break you and some will create you.

Some will be knife for you and some will be spoon .

So now which so ever you are in calm , be grateful, be humble.

Because maybe be this must be yours part but soon time will change .

Because nothing is permanent not even we humans so how can we expect
the things too be permanent.

where so ever you are right now stay clam n enjoy life because it's for only
one time.

Don't end up for toxic people's or toxic situation because you might get free
from ending up but the your own people will be disheartened. .

Don't feel fail if your relationship is not working

Don't feel fail if your work is seen by none

Don't feel fail if you are alone standing opposite to thousands.

Don't feel fail if they cheated on you.

Don't feel fail if they can't see good in you.

Don't feel shame if you have old shoes to start up .

Don't feel fail if you did your best but things don't work out.

Always be sure you are one that no one can ever be....

Every one is not born with golden and sliver spoon .

Some people have to create that spoon.

Because having is good but creating is best.

Nothing is permanent in this world

So how could you expect things to be at same place.

Even the earth is changing its place then we are still human.

No relationship is permanent

No place is permanent

Nothing in this world is permanent expect love.

Chapter8

End.

I hope my words will give you way in life .

I hope my words will give you light and new hope in life.

We all live in society which somehow hurt us or we hurt others but its oki
we all do it.

But most important thing is how you deal with it.

In life nothing is permanent it goes some or other now .

So now that I am ending this I have a little request to you all we are
humans first so spread love and humanity.

If in this there's any thing which hurt some then I am heartily apologizing
it.

All you need to do is be real then being reel for some people .

www.ingramcontent.com/pod-product-compliance
Lightning Source LLC
Chambersburg PA
CBHW020914160726
47993CB00005B/1964